T0142414

The Vocal and Music Artistry

Companion Sheet Music

Cast Your Net Again…
For Such a Time as This

LANA LEE MARLER

ARCHWAY PUBLISHING

Copyright © 2022 Lana Lee Marler.

All rights reserved. No part of this book may be used or reproduced by any means, graphic, electronic, or mechanical, including photocopying, recording, taping or by any information storage retrieval system without the written permission of the author except in the case of brief quotations embodied in critical articles and reviews.

Archway Publishing books may be ordered through booksellers or by contacting:

Archway Publishing
1663 Liberty Drive
Bloomington, IN 47403
www.archwaypublishing.com
844-669-3957

Because of the dynamic nature of the Internet, any web addresses or links contained in this book may have changed since publication and may no longer be valid. The views expressed in this work are solely those of the author and do not necessarily reflect the views of the publisher, and the publisher hereby disclaims any responsibility for them.

Any people depicted in stock imagery provided by Getty Images are models, and such images are being used for illustrative purposes only.
Certain stock imagery © Getty Images.

ISBN: 978-1-6657-1885-1 (sc)
ISBN: 978-1-6657-1886-8 (e)

Library of Congress Control Number: 2022903008

Print information available on the last page.

Archway Publishing rev. date: 03/29/2022

Contents

Amazing Grace 5
https://cast.jacobsladdercdc.org/home/amazing

A Quiet Room* 10
https://cast.jacobsladdercdc.org/home/quiet

There is No I in You* 13
https://cast.jacobsladdercdc.org/home/there

Just* 20
https://cast.jacobsladdercdc.org/home/just

From Love… To Love* 24
https://cast.jacobsladdercdc.org/home/from

His Face* 29
https://cast.jacobsladdercdc.org/home/his

Jesus Said 36
https://cast.jacobsladdercdc.org/home/jesus

Prayer of the Goat 44
https://cast.jacobsladdercdc.org/home/prayer

Amazing Love… How Can It Be* 48
https://cast.jacobsladdercdc.org/home/love

O Holy Vision Most Glorious* 53
https://cast.jacobsladdercdc.org/home/o-holy-vision-most-glorious

*These songs were written with additional instruments. The full scores to these pieces are available upon request by contacting Lana Lee Marler directly at lwmarler@aol.com

Amazing Grace

Lyrics by John Newton
Music: New Britain
Arrangement by Basil Alter

Amazing Grace

Amazing Grace

47
come Tis grace has brought me safe thus
52
rit.
far And grace will lead me home. When
cresc.
Verse 4
a tempo
57
we've been there ten thou - sand years Bright, shi - ning as the
f

Amazing Grace

A Quiet Room

Lyrics by Leslie Weatherhead
Music by Lana Lee Marler
Arrangement by Jeremy Johnson

A Quiet Room

9
now.
And let the cer - tain - ty
11
of your love take a - way my fears.
So let me
14
ris - ing up, now I fol - low
f

A Quiet Room

There is No I in You

Lyrics and Music by Lana Lee Marler
Arrangement by Jeremy Johnson

There is No I in You

There is No I in You

There is No I in You

There is No I in You

There is No I in You

There is No I in You

Just

Lyrics by unknown author and Lana Lee Marler
Music by Lana Lee Marler
Arrangement by Basil Alter

Just

12
a lit - tle child.
Ju - st,
Oh, won't you just,
cresc.
mf
15
How can it be - that "just" is e - nough?
Ju - st,
18
Oh, won't you just,
When the needs of this wor - ld they se - em so tough.
p

Just

21
p
25
Just to be gen - tle, and kind and sweet, Just to be help - ful with
mp
28
3
wil - ling feet, Just to let love be our dai - ly key,

Just

31
That is God's wi - ll for you and me.
Ju - st,
Oh, won't you just,
cresc.
mf
35
It is the Sav - ior whom we - must trust.
Ju - st,
38
rit.
Oh, won't you just,
When we ans - wer His ca - ll to be wil - ling to "just."
p

From Love... To Love

Lyrics and Music by Lana Lee Marler
Arrangement by Basil Alter

From Love... To Love

24
bur - den all for us. Come in our hearts blest Vir - gin's Son, re -
28
deemed by grace, the vic - 'try won. Your love, O God, pur - sues us still; grant that
32
we may do your will.

From Love... To Love

48
rit.
own.
from
love
to
love
Your
a tempo
51
own.
rit.
55

His Face

Lyrics by Helen H. Lemmel and Lana Lee Marler
Music by Lana Lee Marler
Arrangement by Basil Alter

His Face

13
dark-ness I see. But there is light for a look at the Sav-ior, And life more a-
sim.
17
molto rit.
a tempo, sempre molto rubato
bun-dant and free. Turn your eyes up-on Je - sus. Look full in His won-der-ful
mf
21
rit.
a tempo
face; And the things of this world will grow strange - ly dim... In the

His Face

24
Light of His glo - ry and grace.
mp
sfp
29
His word shall not fail me, He pro - mised; Be - lieve Him and
33
all shall be well. Then I will go to a world that is dy - ing,
sim.

His Face

36
rit.
a tempo
His per - fect sal - va - tion to tell. Turn your eyes up - on
mf
39
Je - sus. Look full in His won - der - ful face; And the
42
rit.
a tempo
things of this world will grow strang - ely dim... In the Light of His glo - ry and

His Face

45
♩ = 100, Moving
grace.
mf
50
I feel so ver - y
mp
55
thank - ful; it makes my heart sing. New life I have been

His Face

59
giv - en By the Mak - er of all things. I find it hard to
mf
63
fath - om; it's won - der - ful to know; My
66
sins are all for - giv - en as I look on Je - sus'

His Face

♩ = 80, Much slower, very freely
69
face;
His
face.
72
Face...
His
75
face.
mp
p

Jesus Said

Lyrics from New Testament Gospels Matthew and John
Adapted by Lana Lee Marler
Music by Lana Lee Marler
Arrangement by Robert Totten

Jesus Said

14
me.
I am the good shep - herd. My sheep hear my
rit.
18
voice. I know my own and my own fol - low
mf
22
a tempo
me.

Jesus Said

25
The first and grea - test com - mand - ment is
28
love the Lord your God with all your
31
heart, soul, mind and strength. The

Jesus Said

34
se - cond grea - test com - mand - ment is like the
37
first: To love your neigh - bor
40
as your - self.

Jesus Said

43
As I have
46
loved you love one an - o - ther.
49
This new com - mand - ment is love one - a -

Jesus Said

52
no - ther.
By this shall men know
55
you are my dis - ci - ples
if you have
58
love one for a - no - - ther.

Jesus Said

61
64
By this shall men know you are my dis -
67
ci - ples if you have love one for a -

70
no - ther.
73
rit.
One for a - no -
3
76
ther.

Prayer of the Goat

Lyrics adapted by Lana Lee Marler
from poem by Carmen Benos de Gasztold
Music: Ebenezer Tune composed by Thomas John Williams
Arrangement by Basil Alter

Prayer of the Goat

Prayer of the Goat

Prayer of the Goat

Amazing Love.. How Can It Be?

Lyrics by Charles Wesley
Adapted Lyrics and Music by Lana Marler
Arrangement by Basil Alter

Amazing Love.. How Can It Be?

23
sued.
f
dim.
27
Long my im - pri - soned spi - rit lay Fast bound in sin and na - ture's night;
mp
31
Thine eye dif - fused a quick - 'ning ray, I woke, the dun - geon

Amazing Love.. How Can It Be?

Amazing Love.. How Can It Be?

O Holy Vision Most Glorious

Lyrics and Music by Lana Lee Marler
Arrangement by Basil Alter

O Holy Vision Most Glorious

O Holy Vision Most Glorious

O Holy Vision Most Glorious

O Holy Vision Most Glorious

O Holy Vision Most Glorious

O Holy Vision Most Glorious

O Holy Vision Most Glorious

References

Bonnell, Daniel, 2021. *Cast Your Net,* used by permission of Bonnell, Daniel, 2021, Front Book Cover Art

Newton, J., 1779., Britain, New, Alter, Basil, 2021 *Amazing Grace - Wikipedia.* [online] En.wikipedia.org. Available at: <https://en.wikipedia.org/wiki/Amazing_Grace>, public domain p. 5

A Quiet Room Etchells, R., 2008. *Just as I am.* London: SPCK, p.62-63, Weatherhead, L., 1985. *A Private House of Prayer.* New York: Abingdon Press, p.176, Marler, L. and Johnson, Jeremy, 2021, used by permission of Marler, L. and Johnson, Jeremy, 2021, p. 10

Marler, L. and Johnson, Jeremy, 2021. *There is No I in You,* used by permission of Marler, L. and Johnson, Jeremy, 2021, p. 13

Unknown, Marler, L., Alter, Basil, 2021. *Just,* used by permission of Marler, L. and Alter, Basil, 2021, p. 20

Marler, L. and Alter, Basil, 2021. *From Love … To Love,* used by permission of Marler, L. and Alter, Basil, 2021, p. 24

Lemmel, H., 1922, *Turn Your Eyes Upon Jesus.* [online] Hymnary.org. Available at: <https://hymnary.org/text/o_soul_are_you_weary_and_troubled>, Marler, L. and Alter, Basil, *His Face,* used by permission of Marler, L. and Alter, Basil, 2021, p. 29

Gospels of Matthew and John, New Testament, Marler, L., and Totten, Robert, 2021, *Jesus Said,* used by permission of Marler, L. and Totten, Robert, 2021 p. 36

Gasztold, C., Godden, R. and Primrose, J., 1947 *Prayers From the Ark.* Gasztold, C. and Etchells, R., 2008. *Just as I am.* London: SPCK, p.50. Marler, L., Williams, J. Thomas, and Alter, Basil, 2021. *Prayer of the Goat.* Memphis, used by permission of Marler, L. and Alter, Basil, 2021 p. 44

Wesley, C., 1738. *And Can It Be, That I Should Gain?* [online] [public domain] Hymnary.org. Available at: <https://hymnary.org/text/and_can_it_be_that_i_should_gain> Marler, L. and Alter, Basil, 2021. *Amazing Love...How Can It Be.* Memphis, used by permission of Marler, L. and Alter, Basil, 2021, p. 48

Marler, L. and Alter, Basil, 2021. *O Holy Vision Most Glorious,* used by permission of Marler, L. and Alter, Basil, 2021, p. 53

Hamilton, Julie, 2021. *Stairway to Heaven* used by permission of Hamilton, Julie, 2021, Back Book Cover Art

Printed in the United States
by Baker & Taylor Publisher Services